BASIC BASKETBALL STRATEGY

By HARLEY KNOSHER

Basic Basketball Strategy

FOREWORD BY RICK BARRY

Illustrated with diagrams by Leonard Kessler

DOUBLEDAY & COMPANY, INC., GARDEN CITY, NEW YORK

796.32
K72l.

Library of Congress Catalog Card Number 79-171302
Copyright © 1972 by Rutledge Books, Inc.
All Rights Reserved
Printed in the United States of America

To the coaches who have taught me all the basketball I know and the players who have let me try to teach it to them.

Foreword

I've been fortunate enough to win a number of scoring titles in my life, including ones in the NCAA, the NBA, and the ABA. Although I'm proud of my shooting records, I'm just as proud of my percentage from the foul line, my ability to rebound and to handle the ball or assist a teammate. But it's more than just a matter of having pride in these skills—without them I never could have made a career of basketball.

I was lucky enough to learn basketball the right way when I was growing up. And I knew enough to work hard at learning. Without the right teaching and the desire to work, the odds are against you.

Harley Knosher has been teaching young people to play basketball for a long time. His knowledge of the game is well established. His fundamentals are sound, his explanations clear. In this book, *Basic Basketball Strategy*, Mr. Knosher covers every aspect of basketball strategy that concerns a young player, from basics to advanced techniques, from shooting and dribbling to setting a fast break, switching and gambling on defense.

Basic Basketball Strategy makes you think about your game. It teaches you, for instance, the four things you should consider before taking a shot. Mr. Knosher speaks both from the coach's point of view and from the player's point of view, which will give any reader a more complete understanding of the sport.

Whether you're interested in making a team or just want to improve part of your game, *Basic Basketball Strategy* is the next best thing to a coach.

Rick Barry

Contents

Offensive Strategy

1 The Psychology of Shooting — 3
2 What Shots to Use — 7
3 Three Ways to Dribble — 13
4 Throwing the Right Pass — 19
5 Getting Offensive Rebounds — 25
6 The Set Offense — 29
7 The Pick and Roll — 37
8 The Fast Break — 43
9 The Stalling Game — 49

Defensive Strategy

10 A Defensive State of Mind — 57
11 The Art of Switching — 65
12 Zone Defense vs. Man-to-Man — 69
13 Gambling on Defense — 73

Physical and Mental Preparation

14 Getting into Shape — 81
15 Improving Your Game — 85
16 The Art of Not Fouling — 91
17 Knowing the Rules — 99

BASIC BASKETBALL STRATEGY

1
THE PSYCHOLOGY OF SHOOTING

Developing confidence: Every maneuver made on the basketball court should be directed toward getting the ball into the basket. Every man on the floor must be able to score if he is given a good opportunity; otherwise, he cannot fully justify his position on the team. Of the many elements that contribute to shooting ability, the most important is confidence.

The first step in building confidence in shooting is to learn the fundamental techniques. Your coach can instruct you in proper grip, release, eye contact, and other phases of shooting, but once you have learned these, you must spend hours practicing. Learn to score from many spots on the floor. Work on the shots you will use in games, and develop the touch that will enable you to come through in tense situations. Above all, don't just work on the easy shots. Try the hard ones. Only practice can help you overcome your weaknesses.

Developing concentration: When you feel reasonably confident of your ability to shoot accurately, work on concentration. Don't allow outside distractions to keep you from thinking about the ball and the basket. You might be distracted by your fear of missing the shot or by anticipation of body contact or even by your concern over unfamiliar surroundings. Many players allow themselves to be distracted by loose rims, inadequate lighting, or simply by a larger or smaller gym than they are used to. Anger can be dangerous if you want to be in control. It causes your muscles to tense and tighten up. To be a successful shooter you should be as loose and supple as possible. When shooting, concentrate on the front two inches of the rim. Once you can do this without any distraction, you will be able to reach your full potential as a shooter.

What to consider before shooting: Before taking a shot, consider four things: 1. Do you have good balance? Balance is developed by bringing your feet into a similar position before each shot. To do this you must usually slow down in the last two steps before making the shot. 2. Are you within your own shooting range? You should determine your range by testing it in practice. This is the distance at which you can shoot the ball with adequate arc and without any undo strain. 3. Is the shot one you would expect to make during practice? 4. If you miss, do you and your teammates have at least a fifty-fifty chance for a possible rebound? Practice and actual game situations will teach you to recognize when these questions can be answered positively. Any time they can and your team is not stalling on purpose, don't pass up the shot.

The last step in building confidence is learning not to hesitate when it is your turn to shoot. Don't worry when the ball doesn't go in. If what you are doing is fundamentally sound, you will score your share of points. And remember, even the professionals have off nights.

Tips

1. Learn and practice the fundamentals of good shooting.
2. Be willing to work on weaknesses and ask advice.
3. Don't let anything break your concentration.
4. Learn to identify good opportunities for shooting and take the shots quickly.

2

WHAT SHOTS TO USE

Because basketball has become such a fast game, only three shots are used frequently in the midst of play: the jump shot, the layup, and the hook shot. Foul shots are equally important, and because the player can take his time on these shots, he should make it a matter of pride not to miss.

The jump shot: Younger players who don't have enough strength to use the jump shot can practice the fundamentals of this shot by using a moving one-hand shot. This is accomplished by releasing the ball with one hand while on the run. To shoot correctly, move toward the basket, then jump and release the ball with the fingertips from a point as high off the floor as possible. Keep your eyes on the front two inches of the rim until the ball gets

THE JUMP SHOT: KEEP YOUR EYES ON THE RIM AND FOLLOW THROUGH.

THESE MISTAKES WILL KEEP THE BALL OUT OF THE BASKET.

there. Once you have released the ball, your shooting arm should be completely extended in a follow-through motion.

The layup: The layup is taken very near the basket, usually when a particularly successful offensive move has been made. It is usually a running one-hander that is banked off the backboard into the basket. The shooter is apt to be moving very rapidly, and it is important that he be able to gauge his speed so that he can shoot as he jumps off of one foot. Remember, this should be a high jump, not a broad jump.

THE LAYUP: THE CLOSER YOU ARE TO THE BASKET, THE BETTER.

THIS KIND OF JUMP MAKES THE LAYUP A DIFFICULT SHOT.

As in all shooting, keep your eyes on the spot where the ball will be going. Before the shot is taken, you must decide whether the ball will be banked off the backboard or swished through the basket just over the top of the rim. Once you know where the ball is going, you have only to jump high and get the ball in position to drop quickly through the net.

Learn to shoot the layup from either side of the basket. Use the right hand from the right side and the left hand from the left. This gives you the best banking angle and allows you to keep your body between the basket and your defender. Also, try to find a pattern for this shot so that you can consistently make the same motions.

The hook shot: It is never too early to learn the hook shot. Tall players need it because they will be playing near the basket. Smaller players will find it very helpful when they want to shoot from a crowd.

THE HOOK SHOT: NOTE THE ANGLE OF THE SHOOTER'S STEP AND HOW FAR HE HAS TURNED HIS HEAD.

As you work on hooking, be sure to step at a right angle to a line going from you to the basket. Turn your head early, and look at the basket before you take the shot. Then, bring the ball directly over your head, shoot, and follow through by swinging your whole body toward the basket.

The free throw: Too many players, young and old, forget the importance of the free throw. Many games are won or lost on the strength of a team's foul-shooting ability. First, find a comfortable stance at the foul line. Then relax by taking a deep breath and bouncing the ball a few times. When you have found a shot that works for you, keep it. You should always shoot the foul shot the same way. And, of course, never allow anything to interfere with relaxation or concentration. Be sure to check the rules, and be aware of the various ways you can disqualify your own or a teammate's free throw.

Tips

1. Learn all shots: the jump shot, layup, hook shot, and foul shot.
2. Use the moving one-hand shot until you are strong enough to execute the jump shot properly.
3. Develop a method for shooting layups and then concentrate on getting the ball into the basket consistently.
4. Practice shooting layups from both sides of the basket, using the right hand from the right side, the left hand from the left.
5. To execute a hook shot, step at a right angle from a line from you to the basket and then use your whole body in the follow-through.
6. Remember to be comfortable, relax, and concentrate when taking foul shots.

3

THREE WAYS TO DRIBBLE

When to dribble: Dribbling and passing are the two ways to move the basketball down the court. It is just as important to know *when* to dribble as it is to know *how*. If the ball can be moved with a pass, that should always be your first choice. Never dribble just for show. If you are in a tight situation, try faking and pivoting to create an opening before you dribble, because once you stop dribbling, you must pass or shoot. When an opening is established, you can make the dribble work for you, putting you in a better position to release the ball without letting the other team intercept it.

How to dribble: Dribbling is a controlled motion. Contact with the ball is made with your fingertips. The ball, cushioned on the fingers, rides up with your hand for a brief interval before it is returned to the floor. Never slap or bat the ball.

DRIBBLING: THIS PLAYER HAS CONTROL.

OFFENSIVE STRATEGY

When you dribble, try to keep your body between the ball and your defender. This makes it more difficult for him to knock the ball out of your hands. However, be sure you don't approach the basket with your back to it. Always dribble with your head up. This allows you to look at the basket and keep an eye out for an open man who could receive a pass.

THIS PLAYER DOES NOT.

DRIBBLING WITH YOUR HEAD UP ENABLES YOU TO SEE THE OPEN MAN.

The low-bounce dribble: Dribbling can be useful when your team wants to stall. To eat up the clock while protecting a lead, have the best dribbler keep possession of the ball while his four teammates distract their defenders by staying on the move reasonably far from the dribbler. In this situation, it is important that the man who is dribbling has complete control of the ball and can keep it away from anyone on the opposing team. He should dribble low. By cutting down the distance from your hand to the floor you reduce the chance of error and make it more difficult for an opponent to intercept the ball. The low dribble should be used whenever you are being guarded closely or have more than one defender nearby.

The high-bounce dribble: The high- or long-bounce dribble is used when you want to move the ball as rapidly as possible without passing and when you have plenty of open floor in front of you. Allow the ball to come up as high as your chest and bounce it as far in front of you as you can without losing control of it. The fewer times the ball actually hits the floor, the faster you will move to the basket. Some experienced players use the high dribble as they approach a half-court defense in order to be able to release a pass more quickly when a teammate moves into the open. However, if using the high dribble means you have substantially less control of the ball, don't risk dribbling this way with defenders closing in on you.

USE A HIGH DRIBBLE TO GO AT TOP SPEED.

KEEP THE BALL LOW FOR MAXIMUM CONTROL.

The medium-bounce dribble: Under most conditions, you should dribble with a medium bounce, which allows the ball to come up about belt high, offering a combination of speed and accuracy. With good fingertip control, you can easily switch from a medium dribble to a high or low dribble as the situation on the court changes.

Tips

1. Know when to dribble and when to pass.
2. Dribble with your fingertips, briefly letting the ball ride upward with your hand.
3. Use your body to protect the ball and keep your head up.
4. Dribble low for control.
5. Dribble high for speed.

4

THROWING THE RIGHT PASS

How to pass: A variety of passes are used in any basketball game, but the technique for each pass is fundamentally the same. Always step toward your target as you release the ball, and follow through with your arms and your body to achieve maximum power and accuracy. The ball should reach your teammate somewhere between his belt and his chin; he should not have to lunge at the ball to intercept it. Always throw the simplest pass possible for any given situation. If you can't throw an accurate pass, it is often better not to risk passing. Look for another way to move the ball instead.

The two-hand chest pass: The first pass that most young players learn is the two-hand chest pass. It is generally used to move the ball to an open teammate who is fairly close to you. Sometimes it is thrown in an arc over the head of a defender moving between the passer and the receiver. A key to throwing this pass successfully is holding the ball with your fingers spread and your thumbs together under the ball. The position of your thumbs gives the ball backspin as it is released and makes it easier to catch. To increase the backspin, snap your wrists as you let go of the ball.

THIS PLAYER'S TWO-HAND CHEST PASS IS A GOOD ONE BECAUSE HE HAS PUT BACKSPIN ON THE BALL BY SNAPPING HIS WRISTS.

The two-hand bounce pass: The two-hand bounce pass is used to move the ball into or out of crowded areas. You might want to use it to get the ball to a man who is in position to shoot when there are several defenders around the basket. The bounce pass can also be used for passing to a man who is cutting at the end of a fast break. He will have an improved chance of catching the ball because of the extra fraction of time it takes for the ball to hit the floor and bounce back up to his hands. However, this extra time can also be a disadvantage, so the bounce pass should rarely be used if guards are moving in on the receiver. The safest way to execute a bounce pass is to be sure the ball always hits the floor closer to the receiver than it does to you. The ball should be thrown with backspin, by snapping your wrist and letting the ball slide off your palm.

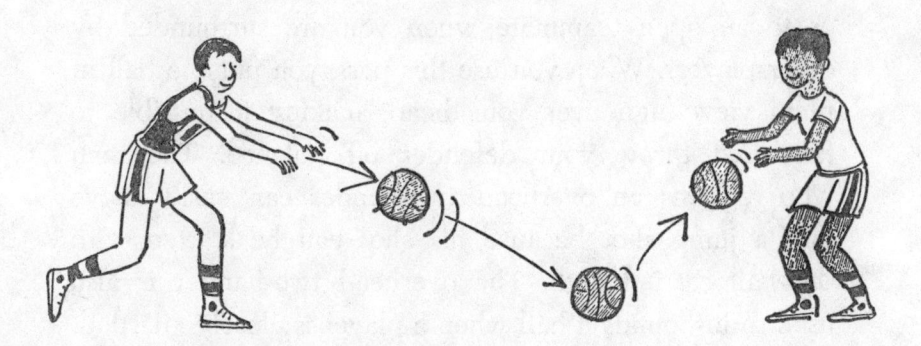

A GOOD BOUNCE PASS WILL BE ON THE WAY UP WHEN IT REACHES THE RECEIVER.

The baseball pass: The baseball pass is just what its name implies, and is used when you want the ball to travel long distances. Be sure to make this a straight overhand shot; otherwise you will find yourself throwing curves, making it harder for your teammates to catch your passes. On a fast break the baseball pass can be used to clear the ball from the defensive basket and hit the open man up the court.

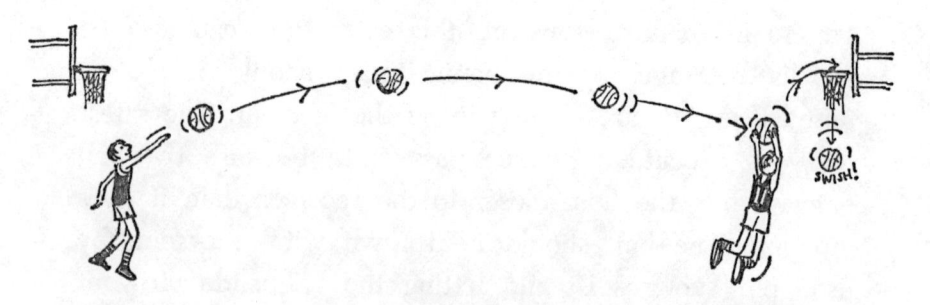

THIS BASEBALL PASS WILL HIT THE MARK BECAUSE IT HAS BEEN EXECUTED WITH THE PROPER OVERHAND MOTION.

The overhead two-hand pass: The overhead two-hand pass can be used to get the ball past a close defender or to an open teammate when you are surrounded by other players. When you use this pass, you put the ball in plain view high over your head, making it possible to fake and throw your defender off balance. The man who receives an overhead two-hander can easily move into a jump shot because his shot can be started with the ball carried high. The overhead two-hander is also used to in-bounds a ball when a player is closely guarded.

Two important things to remember when throwing an overhead two-hander are to snap your wrists for power and to aim a little higher than you actually want the ball to go; you will naturally pull the ball down slightly.

Behind-the-back passes: It is exciting to watch college and professional players throwing passes from behind their backs. The best experienced players throw this kind of pass only when it is appropriate for the situation on the court. Younger players should stick to basic passes until they have enough experience to handle fancy behind-the-back passes.

Catching a pass: For a pass to be completed successfully it must be caught. And catching the ball consistently requires as much work and concentration as the other parts of the game. Whenever possible, step to meet the ball as it comes to you. Let your hands give a little as the ball arrives, and control the ball with your fingertips. Be sure to watch the ball all the way into your hands so that you will have complete control and will not fumble or allow another player to knock the ball away.

PROPER FUNDAMENTALS OF CATCHING INCLUDE MEETING THE BALL, FINGERTIP CONTROL, AND WATCHING THE BALL ALL THE WAY INTO YOUR HANDS.

Tips

1. Learn to throw a variety of passes well, and practice often so that throwing the right pass becomes almost instinctive.
2. In any situation, choose the pass that is most likely to be completed.
3. Put backspin on two-handed passes.
4. Throw the baseball pass straight overhand.
5. Don't use fancy passes until you have mastered the basic ones.
6. Practice so that you can catch as well as you can pass.

5

GETTING OFFENSIVE REBOUNDS

The importance of rebounds: Many teams lose games because they just can't get off enough shots. A team with a strong offense should be able to pick up rebounds and take second and third shots before the opposing team gets the ball. Every minute of practice in getting rebounds will pay off at game time.

Anticipation: You will find that picking up offensive rebounds is easier if you learn to anticipate when your teammates are going to shoot. Study each man's style so that you will have the advantage of knowing before the defender does that a teammate is getting ready to take a shot. Then, once the ball is released, move in an open path to the basket. Many players make the mistake of always taking a straight line to the basket, but this is just the route that will be cut off by an alert defensive team. Your job is to find an opening that will allow you to get in position to grab the rebound. If you are not there as the ball rebounds, you will never have a chance for a second shot.

A GOOD OFFENSIVE REBOUNDER NEVER STANDS STILL.

Timing: Proper timing is essential in intercepting a rebound. You have to learn not to jump too soon or too late. To practice your timing, throw the ball against the backboard again and again, leaning to meet it at the top of your jump with your arms fully extended.

The tip-in: There are several types of offensive rebounds, and a good player should develop the ability to use all of them. The most common rebound is the tip-in. This is a controlled one-handed shot, executed just as you meet the ball at the highest point of your jump. If you can keep the ball on your fingertips for a fraction of a second, you will have better control over its direction. Otherwise, you will be slapping the ball, which will keep it in the air but will probably not send it into the basket.

The catch-and-shoot: Another type of offensive rebound is the catch-and-shoot. When you are in the air or as you return to the floor, catch the ball and quickly take a shot. If you return to the floor before you can release the ball, it is a good idea to try one or two head-and-shoulder fakes, getting the defenders off balance before you shoot. This is especially helpful if the defenders are taller than you are.

Concentrating on the basket: Many coaches believe that you should think of any shot you take as a pass to yourself. Certainly any player who picks up a lot of rebounds by following his own shots aggressively presents special problems to the defenders. One word of caution: Be certain that you are concentrating on the basket and have completed the shot before starting for the rebound. If the effort to rebound causes you to cut short your follow-through or take your eyes off the basket, you will never develop shooting accuracy.

The coach's responsibility: Part of the responsibility for gaining offensive rebounds lies with the coach. The team should have several patterns of attack, coordinating timing, positions, and routes to the basket. A successful offensive strategy should net your team about 40 percent of the available offensive rebounds, but even the best strategy will fail unless each player has a real desire to make it work and contributes his best effort.

Tips

1. Getting offensive rebounds requires teamwork and real effort.
2. Try to anticipate when a shot is being taken.
3. Always take the most open route to the basket.
4. Tip in or shoot whenever possible; slap the ball as a last resort.
5. Follow your own shot only after it is fully executed.

6

THE SET OFFENSE

The importance of the set offense: Every basketball team should be able to carry out a well-planned offensive strategy. The best fast-breaking teams can average only fifteen to twenty baskets a game from their breaks, so they establish set half-court offensive patterns that put them in good positions to score.

Considerations in choosing a set offense: A coach must consider many factors in determining which set offense to use. Is there one outstanding player around whom play can be structured? If so, will he be playing near the basket or at guard or forward? Would it be better to strive for balanced scoring, giving as many men as possible the chance to shoot? Should there be one or two guards on the floor? What kinds of plays will produce opportunities for the shots the team scores with best? To answer these questions a coach must carefully evaluate his players' abilities and the strengths and weaknesses of the opposition.

When a coach develops a set offense, he tries to make it fit the abilities of his players and to keep it as simple as possible. Each player should understand what he is to do on a particular play and should be able to do it. It is, of course, a mistake to teach plays that are too involved for younger players to use under stress or to develop an attack that they are not capable of carrying out.

There are any number of set offensive alignments. Some of the most common are the 1–3–1, 2–3, 1–2–2, and 3–2. (See diagrams.)

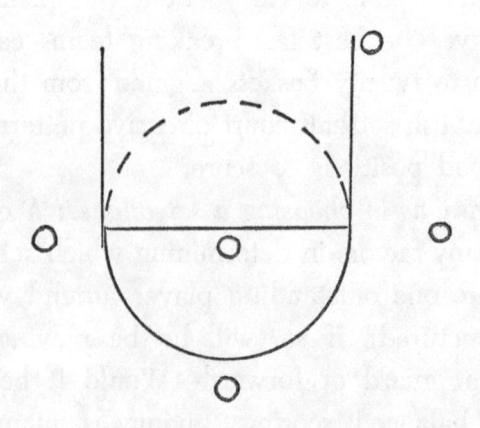

SET OFFENSIVE ALIGNMENTS: 1–3–1

2-3

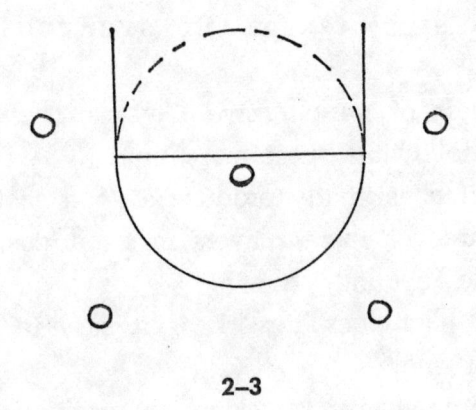

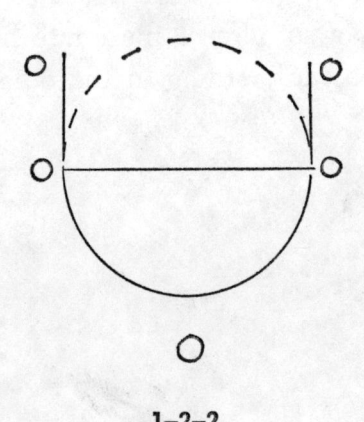

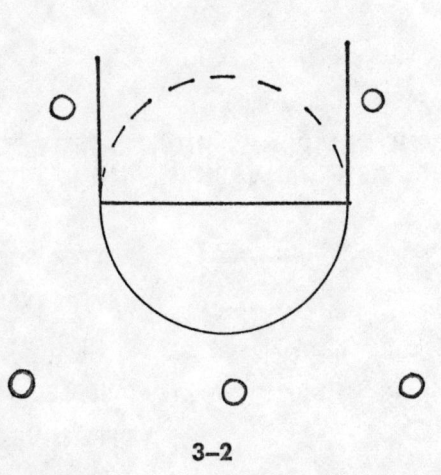

1-2-2

3-2

The success of an offensive play can be judged by asking the following questions:
1. Does it consistently produce a good shot?
2. Are three or more players in good position for a possible rebound?
3. If this play doesn't work, is it easy to move into another one?
4. Is there always someone in position to guard against the opponent's fast break?

To be effective, a set offense must rate high in the first category and be fairly strong in the other three.

THE FOLLOWING DIAGRAMS ILLUSTRATE GOOD OFFENSIVE PLAYS FROM VARIOUS ALIGNMENTS.

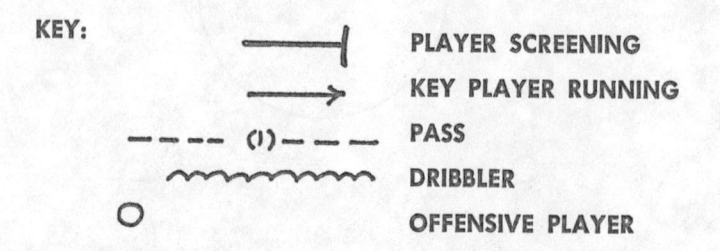

KEY:

———⊣	PLAYER SCREENING
———▶	KEY PLAYER RUNNING
— — (1) — —	PASS
⁓⁓⁓⁓⁓	DRIBBLER
O	OFFENSIVE PLAYER

OFFENSIVE STRATEGY 33

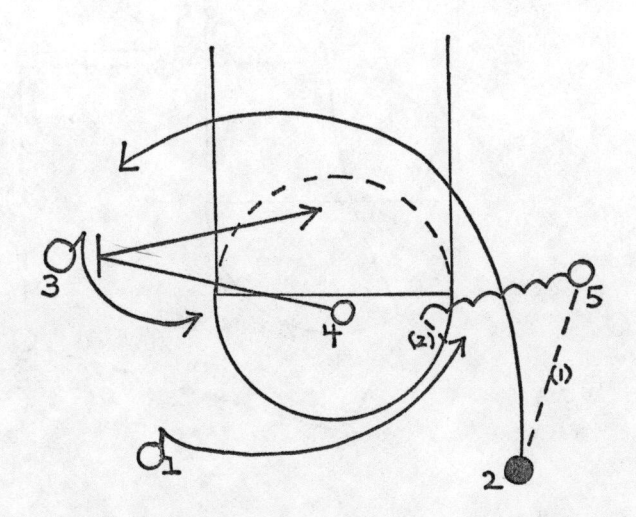

A. 2 PASSES TO 5 AND CUTS THROUGH AND AROUND FOR DEFENSIVE BALANCE.
B. 5 DRIBBLES INTO THE LANE EITHER TO HAND OFF TO 1 OR PASS TO 3.
C. 3 CUTS FOR THE BASKET, USING THE SCREEN SET BY 4.
D. 4 SCREENS AND ROLLS TO THE BASKET FOR THE REBOUND.

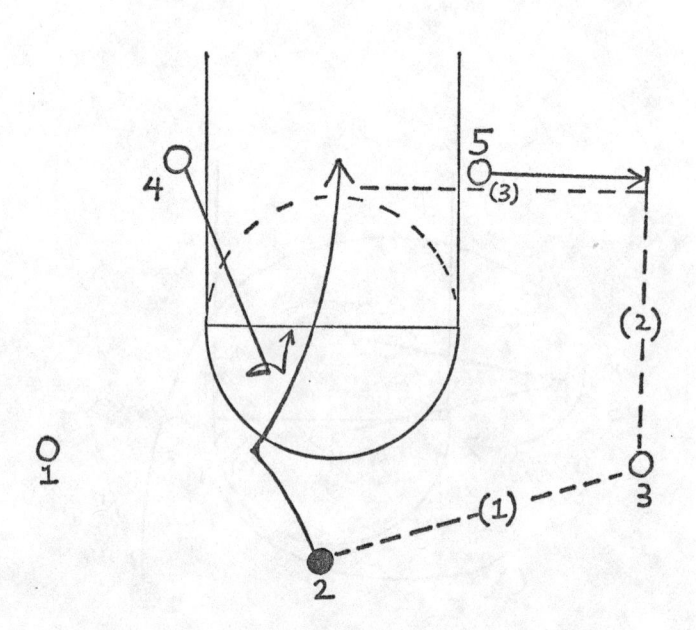

A. 2 PASSES TO 3 AND CUTS OFF THE SCREEN SET BY 4.
B. 3 PASSES TO 5 IN THE CORNER.
C. 5 PASSES TO 2 FOR THE LAYUP OR TO 4 ROLLING BEHIND 2.
D. 1 MOVES BACK FOR DEFENSIVE BALANCE.

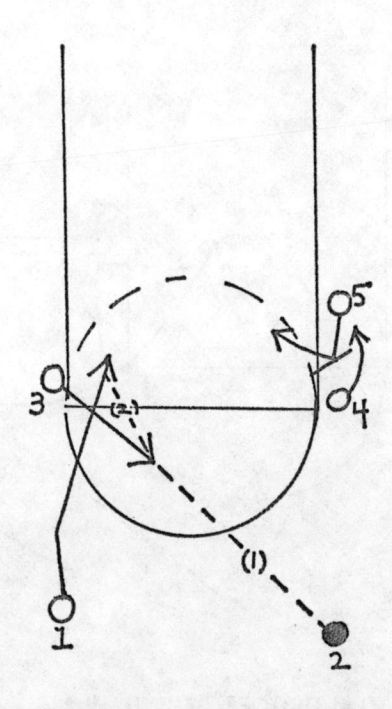

A. 2 PASSES TO 3 BREAKING INTO THE LANE.
B. 3 PASSES TO 1 CUTTING BEHIND HIM FOR THE BASKET.
C. 4 AND 5 EXECUTE A PICK AND ROLL TO KEEP THEIR MEN BUSY AND TO GAIN BETTER REBOUNDING POSITION.

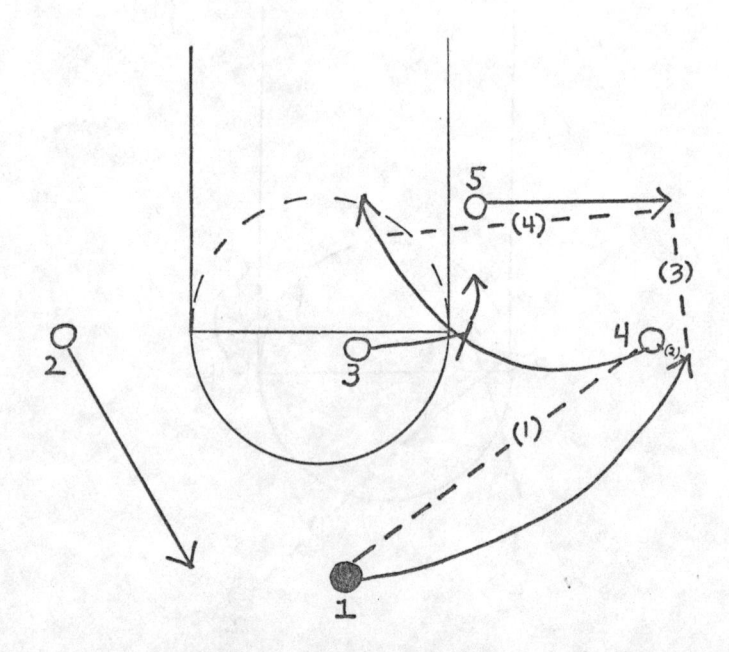

A. 1 PASSES TO 4 AND GOES BEHIND HIM TO GET THE BALL BACK. HE THEN THROWS IT TO 5 IN THE CORNER.
B. AFTER RETURNING THE BALL TO 1, 4 CUTS OVER THE SCREEN SET BY 3.
C. 3 SETS A SCREEN AND ROLLS FOR THE REBOUND OR A POSSIBLE PASS FROM 5.
D. 5 PASSES THE BALL TO EITHER 4 OR 3 FOR THE SHOT.
E. 2 MOVES BACK FOR DEFENSIVE BALANCE.

7

THE PICK AND ROLL

What the pick and roll is: In most set offenses, coaches use a maneuver called the pick and roll. The pick and roll involves two offensive men, called the picker and the cutter, and one man on defense. The picker positions himself in the path of the defensive man, acting as a screen so that his teammate can cut to get away from the defender.

The role of the picker: According to the rules of basketball, if the pick, or screen, is to take place in front of or to the side of the defensive man, it may be set as close as possible as long as the picker does not move into the defender. If the picker is behind the defender, the defender must be given room to turn and take one full step before contact is made. However, screens are most successful when they are set close to the defender, or in other words, to the side or in front.

Once the picker has moved into a screening position, he should stand on the balls of his feet with his knees bent and his hands at his sides. His feet should be set at about shoulder width. He is then in the best position to execute the rolloff, which will free him of the defender and continue to screen the cutter.

It is as important to know when to roll off as it is to know how. An effective rolloff enables a player to be unguarded for a long enough time to *receive a pass*. At the first moment of contact between the defender and the picker, the picker snaps his upper body toward his cutting teammate and takes a backward step in this direction. He completes the roll by taking a quick second step with his other foot, establishing the path to the basket. As he rolls off, the picker must keep his eyes on the cutter and the ball. A good picker never turns his back on the cutter.

The role of the cutter: The cutter should approach a pick situation with an open mind. If he has the ball, he may go up to shoot, continue the drive, or pass the ball to the rolloff man (the picker). To be able to take advantage of all three options, the cutter should be moving fast but be under control. His path should bring him as close as possible to the picker so that the defensive man cannot squeeze between them. If the cutter elects to shoot, he will usually take the shot from right behind the picker. Whenever possible, the cutter should continue driving to force the defense to fall

OFFENSIVE STRATEGY

RIGHT

KEEP YOUR EYES ON YOUR TEAMMATE SO YOU CAN CATCH HIS PASS.

WRONG

NEVER TAKE YOUR EYES OFF THE MAN WITH THE BALL.

back into the basket area and permit a short shot. Often a cutter will throw a pass just before he has released the ball for a shot if he sees that the rolloff man is free. If the cutter is dribbling, he can use a one-hand bounce pass to his teammate to lead the rolloff man to the basket once he has gained a step on the defender.

When the cutter does not have the ball, the pick has been set to open him to receive a pass. Again, it is important to cut as close as possible. If the cutter can use a head-and-shoulder fake before making his drive, the defender is more likely to be stopped by the pick.

Good defensive teams try to stop the pick and roll by putting themselves where the cutter wants to go. The rule to follow in this situation is: Take advantage of what the defense gives you. If the man switching on to the ball is slow, stop and take the jump shot. If he fails to assume a good position, drive for the basket. If the man switching on to the screener is slow, throw him the lob or bounce pass for the easy shot. It is important to take the best option available when coming off a screen.

Why the pick and roll is effective: The pick and roll is an effective offensive maneuver because it usually forces the defense to switch guarding assignments. This can often produce defensive mismatches due to differences in the relative size and speed of the players. The pick and roll also provides opportunities for a team to take advantage of a good driver, jump shooter, or inside man. Although it is fairly easy to execute the pick and roll, it is almost impossible to defend against the play when it is run correctly.

Tips

1. The pick and roll is easy to execute and hard to prevent.
2. The pick should be set as close as the rules will allow.
3. The picker must know *how* to roll and *when* to roll.
4. The cutter should approach the pick with an open mind and be prepared to take whatever option the defense permits.
5. Defenders should learn to recognize a pick situation early and anticipate where the offense wants to go.

8

THE FAST BREAK

What the fast break is: One of the most exciting brands of offensive basketball is the fast break. In this style of play, the offensive team tries to get the ball and at least one more man than the defense down the floor in a hurry. To do so requires precision passing, dribbling, and a willingness on the part of every player to run hard and long.

Why the fast break is used: There are several reasons why coaches select the fast break as a basic attack. It may be because their team has superior size or speed, or because the fast break will work best against a pressing defense a certain opponent likes to use. In any case, there is a right way and a wrong way to run a fast break. It is important to understand your job whatever position you play.

The defensive phase: The first phase of a sound fast break begins while the other team still has the ball. If you are one of the men near the basket, it is your responsibility to be in perfect defensive position so that when the ball is shot you will be able to grab the rebound. You do this by keeping between the basket and the man you are guarding. Time your jump carefully and snatch the ball out of the air as aggressively as possible.

The release phase: Once the ball is in your possession, you are ready to begin the release phase of the fast

ALWAYS TAKE A DEFENSIVE REBOUND WITH TWO HANDS. BE AS AGGRESSIVE AS YOU CAN IN GRABBING THE BALL.

OFFENSIVE STRATEGY

break. The most important part of this phase is to use the least possible time in moving the ball from the crowded area under the basket to an open teammate. The receiving positions are usually taken by the guards, who should be waiting at the sides of the court along the free throw line. If necessary, you may use one or two dribbles to clear the ball, but if at all possible you should pass the ball without any delay. Your pass should go to the guard who is on the side of the court on which you took the rebound.

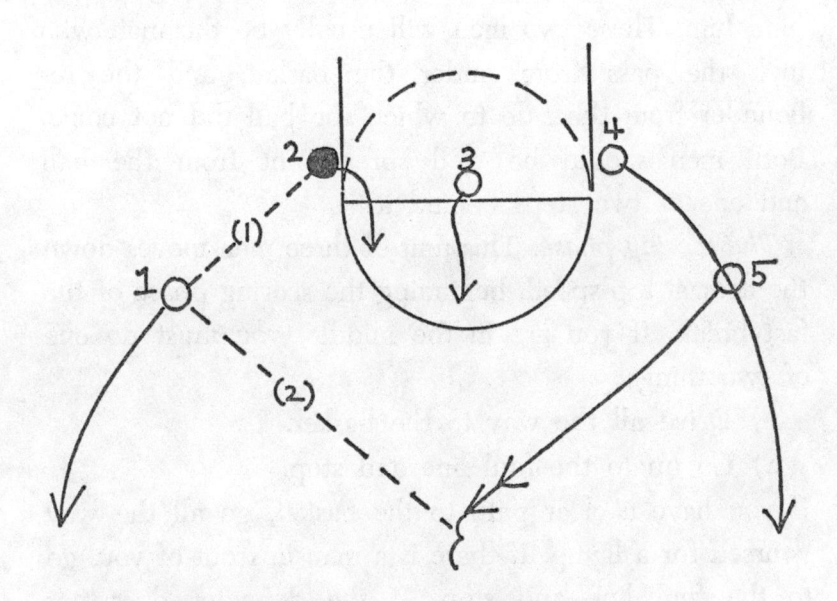

THE FAST BREAK: RELEASE AND MIDCOURT PHASES.
A. 2 TAKES THE REBOUND AND THROWS THE RELEASE PASS TO 1.
B. 1 PASSES TO 5 CUTTING INTO THE MIDDLE AND FILLS HIS OWN LANE ON THE OUTSIDE.
C. 5 TAKES THE PASS AND DRIBBLES DOWN THE MIDDLE.
D. 4, WHO DID NOT REBOUND, RUNS TO FILL THE OTHER OUTSIDE LANE.
E. 3, WHO DID NOT REBOUND, TRAILS THE PLAY DOWN THE CENTER.
F. 2, WHO THREW THE RELEASE PASS, MOVES TO MIDCOURT FOR DEFENSIVE BALANCE.

The man who receives the pass must decide the quickest way to get the ball to midcourt. Ideally he will hit the other guard, who breaks in from the other side. If the other guard is not there, then the receiver may dribble the ball to the midcourt circle himself. But this is less effective, since it wastes time. Once the ball is in the circle, the midcourt phase of the break is in effect.

The midcourt phase: At this point the man in the middle of the court should have the ball and there should be two players, one on either side, slightly behind him. These two men will usually be the man who took the pass from under the basket, and the rebounder from the side to which the ball did not come. Both men should be well spread out from the ball and one or two steps behind it.

The scoring phase: This unit of three men moves down the floor at top speed, beginning the scoring phase of the fast break. If you are in the middle, you must do one of two things:

1) Drive all the way to the basket.
2) Go up to the foul line and stop.

If you have a clear path to the basket, go all the way yourself for a layup. If there is a man in front of you, go to the foul line and stop. If the defender does not challenge you, take a jump shot yourself. If the defender rushes you, pass off to one of your teammates cutting in toward the basket. You should be prepared to shoot. Don't pass off if you are not challenged. If you shoot, follow your shot for a possible rebound. If you pass, stay at the foul line for a possible return pass.

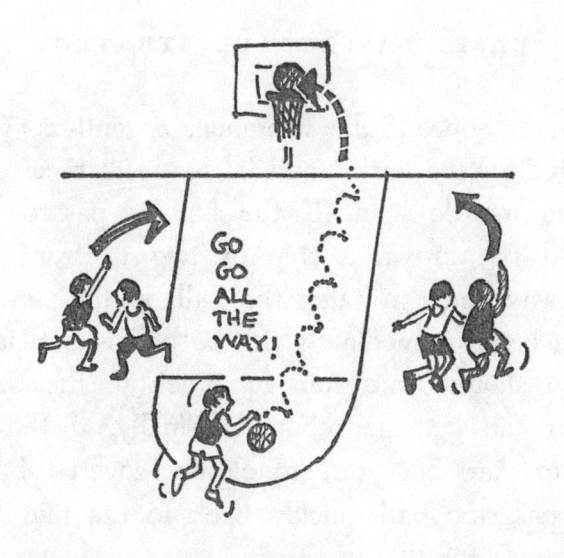

THE FAST BREAK: SCORING PHASE. IF HE CAN, THE MAN WITH THE BALL SHOULD TAKE IT ALL THE WAY.

IF HE IS STOPPED AT THE LINE, THE MAN WITH THE BALL SHOULD SHOOT OR FIND THE OPEN MAN.

If you are one of the wingmen, or cutters, your job is to drive for the basket and be ready to receive a pass from the middle man. If the ball is passed to you, it should be thrown a step or two in front of you. In this way you can catch the ball on the run and go up for a layup immediately. If the ball is not passed to you, you should time your approach to the basket so that you can get the rebound. Finally, if the ball is passed to you, but you are closely covered by a defender, pass the ball quickly back to the middle man; then prepare for the rebound.

A well-run 3-on-1 or 3-on-2 fast break should always result in a good shot. You are trying for the layup, but against expert defenders you may have to settle for the jump shot from the foul line. If the fast break doesn't seem to be working, don't take a wild shot. Wait for the rest of your offense to get downcourt and set up another play.

Tips

1. You must have good defensive position to start a fast break.
2. Release the ball from under the defensive basket as soon as possible.
3. Be sure the ball is in the middle once you reach midcourt.
4. If you are not challenged at the foul line, take the shot yourself unless a teammate is free for a layup.
5. As a wingman, work on timing your break for the basket.

9

THE STALLING GAME

The semistall and the deep freeze: The stalling game is a minor but important aspect of offensive basketball. Most teams do not stall too often or for any great length of time, but when a stall is used, it must work. There are two types of stalls, the semistall and the complete stall or deep freeze. In both cases the idea is to use up more time than usual before giving up the ball. A team using the semistall runs the regular offensive patterns, simply waiting for a better shot than usual. In the complete stall a team tries to maintain possession of the ball as long as possible, using special stalling maneuvers and shooting only when there is an extremely good chance that the shot will score. This is especially true when the score is close. Being sure of the last shot is a defensive as well as an offensive weapon because the opponent cannot score when you have the ball.

Why teams stall: Teams stall for several reasons. Key players may be in foul trouble. Or it may be important to take the last shot of a given period. Stalling can also effectively break momentum built up by the opposition. If a team feels it is completely overmatched, keeping the ball away from the opposition could be the best strategy for victory. Frequently, when it is late in the game and one team leads by a good margin, that team will use up the remaining time by stalling to make sure that its lead is not challenged.

How to stall effectively: There are a few general rules that can help make any stall successful. Team and individual discipline are important in all phases of basketball, but never more than in the stalling game. Communication between coach and squad must be clear, and every player must understand what stalling means and must follow all orders exactly. Since the object of stalling is to maintain possession of the ball and use up time, it is important not to lose the ball through a violation, such as traveling or double dribbling, or because of a bad pass. If a team is stalling, it should only shoot when the chance of making a basket is very good.

It is crucial to keep the clock running, so a stalling team should never commit personal fouls. Anything that stops the clock is damaging when you are trying to stall, and the last thing you want is to let your opponents score without using up time.

If the stall is working well, the stalling team will be

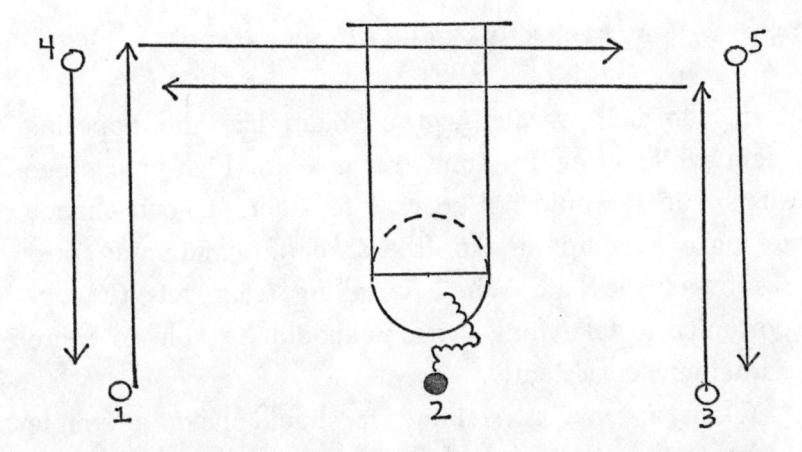

STALLING PATTERN: 1, 4, 3, and 5 CONTINUALLY EXCHANGE POSITIONS ALONG THE SIDELINE AND THE BASELINE. 2 DRIBBLES, MAINTAINING POSSESSION UNTIL HE IS FOULED, GETS A LAYUP, OR IS FORCED TO PASS. THE MAN HE PASSES TO BECOMES THE DRIBBLER. THIS WORKS BEST AGAINST TEAMS USING A MAN-TO-MAN DEFENSE.

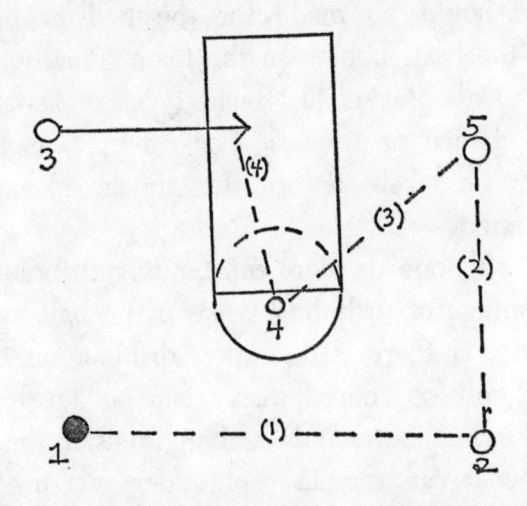

STALLING PATTERN: ALL FIVE MEN KEEP THEIR POSITIONS, THROWING THE BALL AROUND UNTIL SOMEONE HAS A CHANCE TO CUT BEHIND HIS MAN FOR A PASS AND EASY SHOT. THIS WORKS BEST AGAINST A ZONE DEFENSE.

trying to increase its lead or neutralize the opposing team while using up time. Layups are high-percentage shots, and it would not be wise to ignore a good chance to make a layup just for the sake of maintaining possession of the ball. When a stalling team gets the opportunity to take foul shots, it should be able to score with them consistently.

When a team is stalling, it should have a simple plan for the movement of five men and the ball, which hopefully will produce high-percentage scoring opportunities. These plans should hold to a minimum the number of times the ball may be lost. They should provide for maneuvers that will work against man-to-man defenses and against zone defenses. Provision must be made for additional scoring, so whenever possible the basket area should be left clear. Insofar as possible, provision should be made for the ball to be in the hands of the best shooter on the team. Finally, it should be clear to all players just what types of shots provide the best chance of success. For example, can a short jump shot be taken, or are the players to wait for a clean layup?

Teams with one or more outstanding dribblers should take advantage of dribbling to keep the ball away from the defense. If there is no expert dribbler on the team, stalls that rely on sharp passing can be developed.

Usually when a team is stalling, tension builds, and a player who can remain cool under pressure is especially valuable. The player who not only stays cool but also influences his teammates to keep their heads is the man every coach hopes to find. Your ability to remain in control under pressure is increased by the confidence you gain from knowing both how to stall and why.

Tips

1. A successful stall requires clear communication between the coach and the team and cooperation among teammates.
2. A stalling team should never stop the clock.
3. A stalling team should take advantage of good opportunities to score.
4. Knowing how and why to stall helps you keep calm under pressure.

Defensive Strategy

10

A DEFENSIVE STATE OF MIND

Why defense is important: Any man who can make a basketball team should be capable of playing defense well. Speed, quick reflexes and experience certainly help, but the main factor in good defense is desire. A player who really wants to stop an offensive man can do so most of the time.

Defensive ability is particularly important because this is one aspect of play that can remain stable over the course of a season. Every team will occasionally have a bad shooting night. Faulty ball handling or poorly timed offensive patterns sometimes occur for no appar-

58	BASIC BASKETBALL STRATEGY

ent reason, but the player or team that achieves real defensive efficiency should be able to maintain it throughout the year.

A team that is strong defensively can win victories over physically superior teams. Very few teams face aggressive, well-executed defense from their substitute squads during practice, making it harder to deal with a strong defense in actual game situations. A good defen-

NEVER LET YOUR MAN GO TO THE BASKET WITH THE BALL.

sive man is an asset on any team, and all players should master the fundamentals of defensive play.

Defensive position: It is not always a good idea to stay between your man and the basket. If the man you are guarding does not have the ball, it is often better to stay between him and the ball than between him and the basket, concentrating on his moves and reacting to them quickly.

NEVER LET YOUR MAN BEAT YOU TO THE BALL.

MOVE STRAIGHT BACK ON ANY FAKE YOUR MAN MAKES AS LONG AS HE HAS HIS DRIBBLE.

When you are guarding the man with the ball, the basic defensive position is to keep your knees bent and your weight slightly forward on the balls of your feet. Your back should be fairly straight, your head up, and your eyes on the opponent's chest. From this position, your first reaction to any move he makes is to jump straight back about eighteen inches. This enables you to maintain a position between the offensive man and the basket.

If your opponent stops dribbling, move in as close as possible without committing a foul. When he goes up to shoot, you should wait until his feet leave the floor and then make your own leap with your arms fully extended to block the shot. By waiting, you avoid being fooled by a fake jump.

Until you jump to block a shot, the position of your hands and arms should be a matter of comfort. If the offensive man passes instead of dribbling or shooting, try to keep your position between him and the ball.

Sizing up your opponent: In any defensive situation, the defender must judge his own speed in relation to his opponent's. The best guarding position is one that keeps the defensive player as close as possible to the man he is guarding but enables him to move with his opponent so that a good position will not be lost. The guarding distance varies from game to game and man to man, but a good defender will learn to gauge his best position quickly.

As a defender, try to discover your opponent's favorite moves early in the game. If he likes to drive to the right, take a position forcing him the other way. If the outside shot is his best, close in and take away this option. An alert player can learn his opponent's habits during the course of play, but scouting an opponent's moves before the game starts can also be very valuable.

How to play defense: The offensive man's position on the court is an important factor in judging your own moves. If he and the ball are seventy-five feet from the basket, he is not particularly dangerous and you can guard loosely. A good twenty-foot jump-shooter presents an increasing threat with every step he takes past the midline. And any player must be guarded aggressively in the immediate basket area.

Two additional elements that influence decisions made by defensive players are the game score and the time

THIS MAN JUMPED AT THE RIGHT TIME.

on the clock. Knowing the game situation enables a smart defender to make sensible choices. If a player knows his team is several points ahead and there is only a short time left, he will play more conservative defense to avoid stopping the clock with a foul. All normal rules of defense may have to be abandoned if time is about to run out in a losing cause. In this case the necessity of gaining

THIS MAN JUMPED TOO SOON.

possession of the ball may dictate doing everything short of fouling. In special cases, it can even be advisable to foul. The coach will then tell you to go for the ball and either get it or cause contact. This is a good play when the only way your team can win is to stop the clock in hopes of gaining possession and scoring the necessary points.

Tips

1. Desire is one of the most important factors in good defense.
2. Figure out your own ideal defensive position and play it.
3. Learn everything you can about how the man you are guarding plays.
4. Always keep aware of the score and the time left in the game.

11

THE ART OF SWITCHING

What the switch is: A switch is a defensive maneuver in which two or more men exchange guarding assignments. Once a switch has been made, the new assignment is kept until there is an appropriate opportunity to switch back. Switching normally takes place when a defender has lost or is about to lose a favorable position on his opponent. It is important to know when to switch and to be able to communicate with your teammate so that he will know exactly what to do.

Why the switch is used: For many years it was possible to play good man-to-man defense without switching. Many teams still switch only when it is absolutely necessary, but two things make it impractical to stay with the strict man-to-man defense all the time. The first is that many players have perfected the jump shot, which allows a player to get away an outside shot very quickly. Second, coaches are running much more complicated offenses against which a defender may be picked or screened two or three times in one play sequence.

When to execute the switch: The responsibility for initiating a switch belongs to the man guarding the picker, because he is usually in the best position to see what the opposition is doing. If it looks as though a pick is going to be set, he should yell a warning. When the pick is set, he should yell either "switch" or "slide" depending on whether he wants to switch men or simply alert his teammate. Remember that a switch should never be made unless it is called, and if it is called it must be made. Sticking to this rule eliminates a great deal of confusion.

How to execute the switch: If the pick is a good one and a switch is necessary, the man guarding the picker yells "switch" and at the same time quickly moves into the path of the cutter. The idea is to force a change in the cutter's direction, to draw a charging foul, or to make the cutter stop his dribble. In all three cases the offense will be hurt by not being allowed to follow through on the play pattern. Once the cutter's intended path is blocked, the defender must move back into a normal defensive position and be ready for whatever defensive problems arise.

When the man guarding the cutter hears the pick warning, he should be prepared to follow the next command quickly. If it is "slide," his job is to maintain

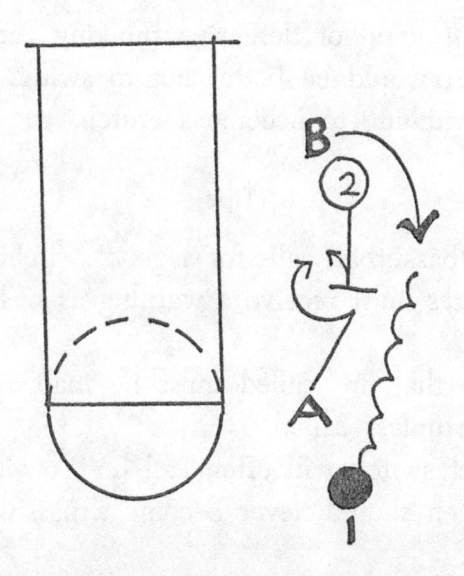

THE SWITCH: OFFENSIVE MAN 1 TAKES DEFENDER A INTO THE PICK SET BY 2. B WARNS A OF A "PICK LEFT" AND WHEN HE SEES THAT IT WILL BE EFFECTIVE, GIVES THE COMMAND "SWITCH." AT THIS POINT B MUST JUMP OUT AND STOP 1, AND A MUST MOVE INTO A POSITION TO STOP A SUCCESSFUL ROLL-OFF BY 2.

perfect defensive position on the cutter. If the call is "switch," it is vital that he drop in behind the picker so that the roll-off move will not enable the picker to beat the defense to the basket. From this new position the defender can also be ready to make a switchback move if the cutter changes direction and comes back over the pick.

The switch is a very aggressive move. It calls for the defensive players to take the initiative. This can be accomplished effectively only if the offense is prevented from going in the direction it wants to go. Too many players think of switching as a passive move. Many try to use the switch to make up for a mistake or for laziness. This kind of defensive thinking can only lead to failure. It would be better not to switch at all than to allow switching to become a crutch.

Tips

1. Modern basketball calls for a good switching defense.
2. Teammates must receive a warning as well as a command.
3. Switches that are called must be made and cannot be made unless called.
4. A perfect switch will often call for a switchback.
5. The switch should never become a passive move.

12

ZONE DEFENSE VS. MAN-TO-MAN

In zone defense the position of the defender is dictated primarily by the ball. In man-to-man defense the defender's position is directly related to that of the man being guarded. When the ball moves, every man in the zone moves accordingly. In man-to-man play, movement of the ball may or may not affect all five defenders. Players in a zone are responsible for an area on the court and any man who comes into it. Man-to-man defenders follow their responsibility everywhere he goes. If these differences are kept in mind, it will be easier to understand the importance of each type of defense.

The zone defense: Zones are usually discussed in terms of number sequences like 1–3–1, 1–2–2, or 2–3. These numbers refer to the position of the five men playing the zone. When a zone defense is in operation, players make shifts depending on the location of the ball. These shifts are made by men moving to the outside of

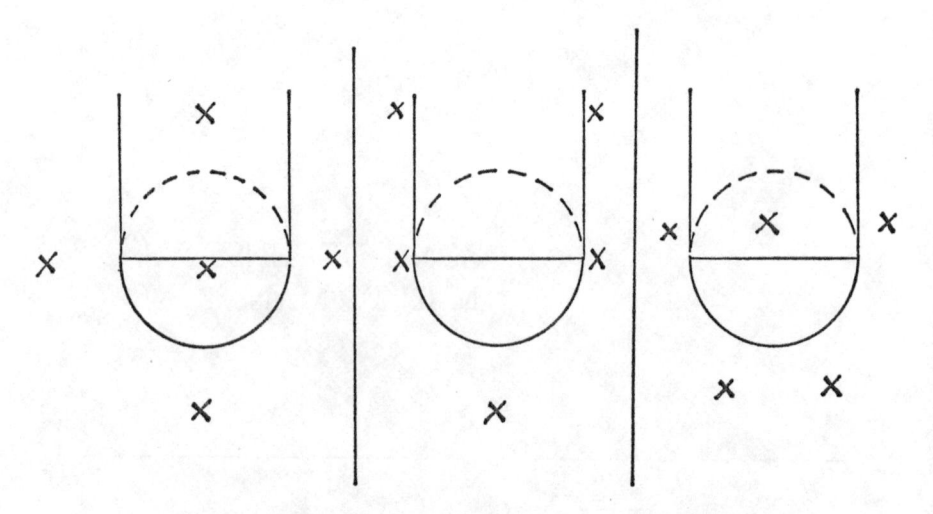

ZONE DEFENSIVE ALIGNMENTS: 1–3–1, 1–2–2, AND 2–3.

the basket on the ball side and down and in toward the basket on the side away from the ball. In this manner several men are generally massed in the lane. The main objective is to keep the ball away from the basket area. To keep up with the ball as these shifts are made is very difficult. It requires a good understanding of the job to be done and lots of hustle. A well-run zone offense will destroy a zone defense that isn't working hard all the time.

When to use a zone defense: There are several situations that lead a coach to select a zone defense. A zone defense is useful when there is no way to adequately match the defenders against the members of the opposing team. This may be because the opponents are too tall, too quick, or too strong. Another good reason to zone is to keep one or two strong rebounders near the basket. Zoning can also help protect one or more players who are in foul trouble, as there is less chance of fouling when a zone is in effect. Zones are are often applied against teams that do not have strong outside shooting, since a zone defense forces the opponents to shoot from a distance. There are also times when a team's offensive patterns are so successful that zoning is the best way to stop them, breaking up the opponents' normal style of play. One great inside player may be enough to cause a team to zone. This is especially true if there is no big man on the defensive team who can stop the inside player.

The offensive advantage of a zone: There is one offensive reason why some teams use the zone. This is to maintain men in positions where they will be ready to run the fast break. By keeping rebounders near the basket and quick run-and-shoot men out on the court, the fast-break team is always ready to follow up on a rebound.

The dangers of a zone: On the negative side, zone defenses sometimes tempt the defenders to relax and to rely too much on the other defenders. Another potential weakness is the fact that no individual assignments can be made. If it is not possible to match individual defensive strength against individual offensive strength, everything depends on the entire team reacting correctly to the position of the ball. Finally, a problem arises about protecting the defensive backboard. Although rebounding position is good, it is hard to keep offensive rebounders off the boards because they have more freedom to maneuver as they please.

The match-up zone: However, there is a good way to realize the advantages of the zone without giving up too much. Every player should learn man-to-man fundamentals and be able to execute them. Once this is accomplished, a method can be found to use man-to-man fundamentals within a zone framework. This is usually done by applying what is commonly called a match-up zone. In this type of defense the players wait for the offense to fill its positions and then shift into positions that enable them to utilize man-to-man principles. The man-to-man fundamentals always apply when guarding a man with the ball or when a zone position away from the ball is being filled. Most important, remember to keep working every minute on defense.

Tips

1. In a zone, the players must always be aware of the location of the ball.
2. Playing a zone well requires as much hustle as man-to-man defense.
3. Zones are useful to overcome defensive problems.
4. The weaknesses of the zone can be limited by applying good man-to-man fundamentals.

13

GAMBLING ON DEFENSE

Why teams gamble: A gambling defense is one in which a team leaves one or more men partially or completely unguarded in order to put extra pressure on the man with the ball. Gambling defenses are normally associated with the closing minutes of a game. However, some teams use them during the entire game. Behind every gambling defense there is one basic idea: to break the opponents' concentration and their offensive patterns. There are many different kinds of presses or gambling defenses which, like general defense, fall into two categories: man-to-man and zone. Presses can be applied over the entire court or may begin at the half-court or three-quarter-court mark. In any case, to be successful the gambling defense must be good at its basic responsibilities.

Putting pressure on the man with the ball: One responsibility is to put heavy pressure on the man with the ball. This can be done by one man or two. A two-man pressure attack is normally a sign of a zone-type press because the remaining four men must be guarded by three, forcing them to do so by areas rather than by specific men. Whether it is applied by one man or two, this pressure must be sufficient to keep the man with the ball from concentrating on the job at hand. The

AN EFFECTIVE DOUBLE TEAM WILL PUT REAL PRESSURE ON THE OPPONENT.

ball handler must not be allowed to pick his spot for a pass or to break the pressure with a dribble. The degree of success of the pressure applied by any one man has a direct bearing on the success of the other men involved in the press, the interceptors, and the basket protector.

The role of the interceptors: There are two or three interceptors. Their function is similar to that of a defensive halfback in football. When pressure is being applied, the interceptor takes a position in anticipation of a pass in order to try to steal it. From this position certain keys will help determine where the pass is likely to go. Where are the receivers? Which way is the passer facing? Are his hands and feet set for a long pass or a short one? Which pass would help the offense most? Each of these clues may give the interceptor a jump.

The role of the basket protector: Another responsibility of the gambling defense is to protect the basket. The gambling defense must not allow cheap baskets to be made very often. To guard against this, one man must move to the basket whenever the opposition brings the ball into the forecourt. The job here is to force the deepest shot possible and never to give away a layup. This requires the use of arms, legs, and voice to throw the attackers off balance. Help will be on the way, so you should force the offense to take as much time as possible.

Choosing a press: Which type of press to use depends on several things. If the opposition is stalling, a zone-type press will force the game more. Examples of these are the 1-2-1-1, the 2-2-1, and the 2-1-2. If game-long, nagging pressure is desired, a full-court man-to-man may be best. Teams with limited over-all speed should consider half-court pressure because there is less court to cover.

Most teams equip themselves with more than one press so that various situations can be dealt with successfully.

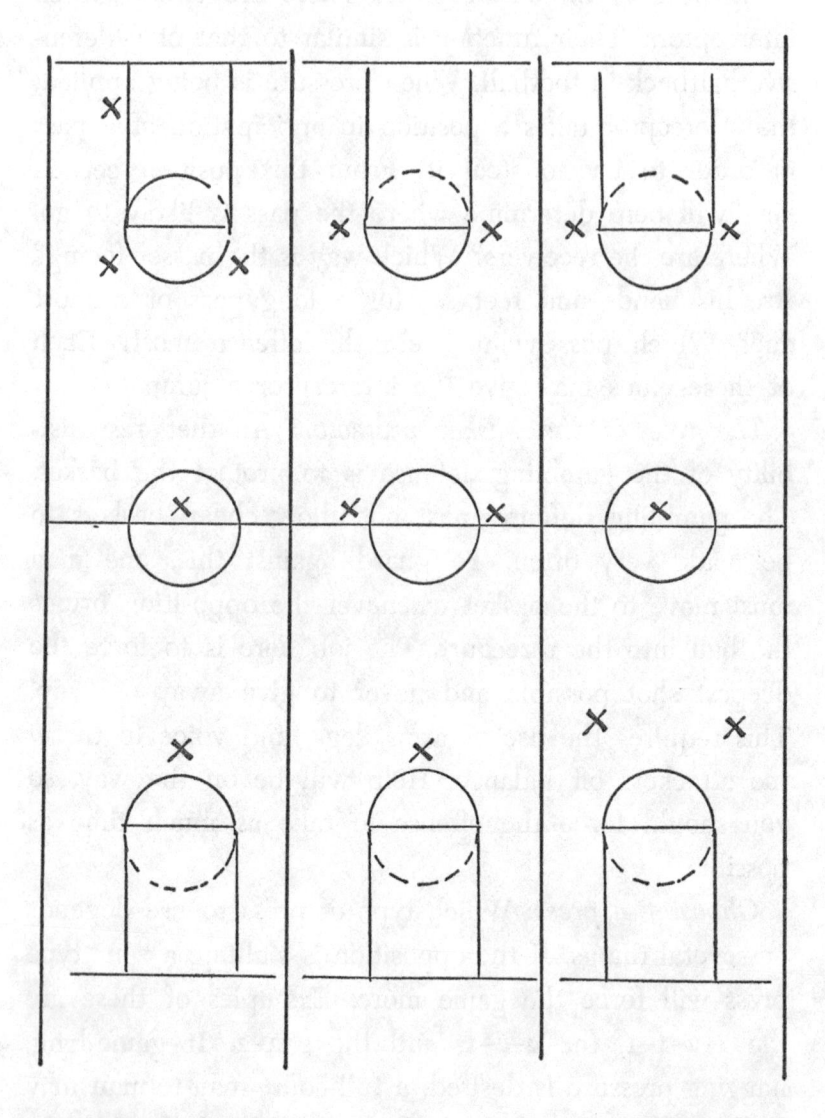

EXAMPLES OF PRESSES: THE 1–2–1–1, THE 2–2–1, AND THE 2–1–2.

As in every phase of basketball, the chances of the various presses working depend on the understanding and desire of the players. Nothing in the game is more demanding than a gambling press. Remember, a gambling press is normally used at the end of a long game. Only players in the best physical shape can run the gambling defense as it should be run.

Individual gambling: Individual players are often capable of gambling on their own during the course of a game. The coach will tell a player with quick hands just what chances can be taken. In general, the farther the defender is from his basket, the more risks he can take.

Steals can often be made by studying the opponents' ball-handling habits. If a cross-over dribble is made high, it can be stolen. If the dribbler is weak with the left hand, force him to dribble on his left. Sneaking in behind a teammate's man often results in a steal. Finally, passes can be broken up by pretending to be loosely guarding a man, then timing a cut just as the passer releases the ball. All of these tricks not only force the opponents to relinquish the ball but also give your team a tremendous psychological lift.

Tips

1. Gambling defenses consist of putting pressure on the man with the ball, using interceptors and protecting the basket.
2. Interceptors should use keys to anticipate where the ball will be thrown.
3. Avoid giving away layups.
4. The coach will tell individuals when and how to gamble on their own.

Physical and Mental Preparation

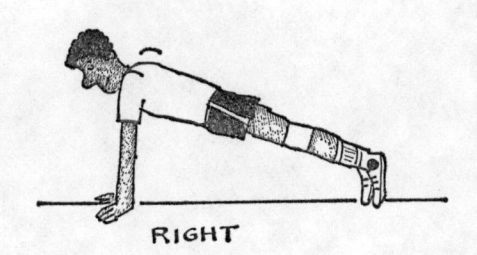

RIGHT

14

GETTING INTO SHAPE

The importance of conditioning: Basketball is one of the most physically demanding of all sports. The action is continuous—at any one time you may be asked to go top speed for two or three minutes, running, stopping, starting, jumping. Your heart, lungs, and legs must be in excellent shape for this kind of activity. The team that can go at full speed late in the game will generally be a winner.

Throughout the entire year and especially during the season, it is important to eat a balanced diet and get adequate sleep. Your coach will tell you how much sleep you need. Preseason workouts should include exercises that will develop speed, endurance, and increased spring and strength.

Speed and endurance: To gain speed you must run sprints. Endurance is developed by running distances, pushing yourself a little harder each day.

Spring: Spring can be increased by using simple toe-rising exercises. Place your toes on a two-by-four piece of wood and push yourself up as high as you can 150 times. Fifty repetitions should be done with the toes pointed out, fifty with the toes turned in, and fifty with the toes straight ahead.

THE RISE ON TOE EXERCISES WILL GO A LONG WAY TOWARD HELPING YOU DEVELOP MAXIMUM SPRING.

General body strength: General body strength can be increased by three basic exercises: pushups, pullups, and situps. There is a right way to do each. When doing pushups be sure not to allow your body or legs to touch the floor, and always keep your back straight. Pullups should be done on a bar that allows you to hang straight down. Do some with your palms out and some with your palms in. Be sure to let yourself all the

RIGHT

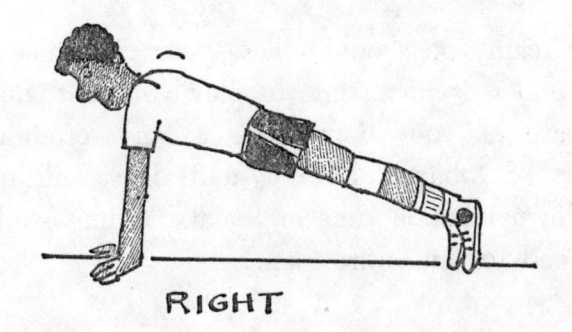

IF EXERCISES ARE GOING TO HELP YOU THEY MUST BE DONE CORRECTLY.

WRONG

way down every time and to pull up until your chin is above the bar. Situps should be done with your feet up under you as far as they will go. Keep your feet firmly planted on the floor, and be sure to sit up all the way on each attempt.

The number of repetitions of these exercises you will be able to do will vary from player to player. If you are to benefit from them they must be done regularly, and repetitions should steadily increase.

Many coaches encourage their players to do these and other exercises with weights. This can be very beneficial but should not be attempted without adequate supervision.

Training rules: Almost every coach has his own approach to training rules, and if you're going to play on the team you should follow your own coach's rules. In general it is impossible to play your best unless you take care of your body. This means refraining from the use of tobacco, alcohol, and drugs, all of which slow down reaction time and make it impossible to go full speed for an entire game.

Tips

1. Top-flight conditioning is a year-'round job.
2. Exercises are useful only if done regularly.
3. If you do an exercise do it right.
4. You can't play consistently at your best unless you care for your body.

15

IMPROVING YOUR GAME

The importance of practice: Although basketball is a team sport, there are many things you can do to improve your own game. Practice whenever possible, both on and off the court. Skills perfected by long hours of individual practice will serve you well in competition and give you confidence in your ability to perform under stress.

Practicing shooting: It is usually most fun to practice shooting. Begin with close shots and move farther from the basket as your muscles warm up. You will soon develop consistency on familiar shots and will be able to spend some time each day working on shots that are new or that are especially difficult for you. Always concentrate on applying the proper fundamentals when you shoot. If your approaches and follow-through are correct, you will begin to make baskets regularly.

Golf: One excellent shooting drill is called "golf." You start out shooting from the first of nine spots and move to the second only after you have made the first shot successfully. The object is to hit from all nine spots in as few shots as possible.

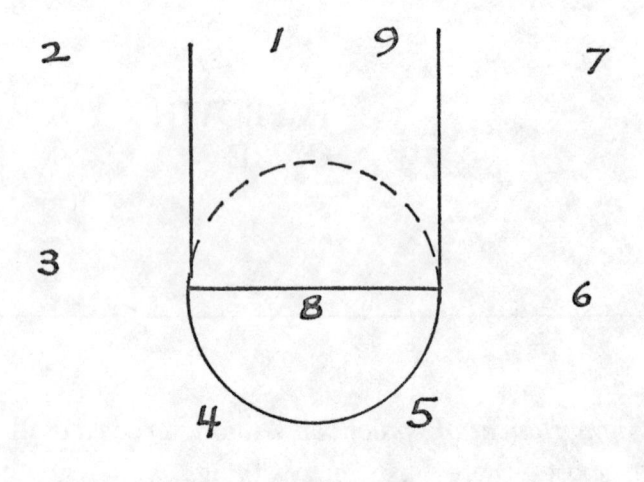

THE POSITIONS FOR GOLF.

The hook-shot drill: Another drill is the continuous hook-shot drill. Start close in on one side of the basket and try a hook shot. As the ball comes through the net, grab it and move into a hook from the other side, using the proper hand from each side. The drill continues as long as the shots are made, and the player keeps track of the greatest number of hits in a row.

Practicing foul shots: The key to practicing foul shots is always to shoot for accuracy rather than speed. It is a good idea never to shoot more than twice in a row without stepping away from the line, since you will never have the opportunity to shoot more than twice in a row in a game situation. You can expect to make 90 percent of your foul shots during practice once you have discovered the stance and motions that make this shot easiest for you.

Dribbling drills: A number of tricks can be used to add variety to dribbling drills. Some coaches advocate wearing gloves and blinders to help you develop a sure sense of touch and perfect control without looking at the ball. Whenever you dribble, keep your head up as if looking for an open teammate or a threatening defender.

"Follow the circles" is a dribbling drill that gives you plenty of chance to change directions and hands. At top speed, dribble around all the circles on the gym floor (including the small center circle), always keeping the ball in your outside hand.

An excellent way to practice controlled dribbling is to place folding chairs about four feet apart and dribble between them. You must stay low, trying to move the length of the row without knocking down the chairs. As your dribbling skills improve, move the chairs closer together and increase your speed.

The "stop-and-go drill" combines dribbling for speed and control. Start at the end line and dribble at top speed to the foul line. At the foul line come to a full stop, still maintaining the dribble. Repeat this process at each of the lines until you reach the far end of the floor.

IN THIS DRIBBLING DRILL TRY TO INCREASE YOUR SPEED WITHOUT LOSING CONTROL OF THE BALL.

Ball-handling drills: Passing and catching can be practiced almost anywhere. You can draw targets on a wall and practice throwing a variety of passes at the targets. As the ball rebounds off the wall, catch it, using all of the proper fundamentals.

Another excellent ball-handling drill is moving the ball as rapidly as possible around your body and your legs. This is the kind of drill the Harlem Globetrotters use in a warmup; it will give you the good hands vital to an outstanding player.

Rebound drills: Offensive rebounds are easier to practice than defensive rebounds. The best drill to develop skill as a tipper can be practiced against a backboard or any wall. Throw the ball against the board and then leap to tip it with your right hand. If there is no basket available, continue tipping until you lose control. If you are using a basket, make sure your last tip goes through the net. When you feel you have improved your skill with your right hand, repeat the drill with your left.

Another good offensive rebounding drill is shooting and intercepting the ball before it hits the floor. Follow your shot whether or not the ball goes through the basket. As soon as you recover the ball, shoot again.

To practice defensive rebounding, use a medicine ball of four, six, or eight pounds. Throw the ball up against a backboard or wall and then jump for it. The practice gained in snatching down the medicine ball will prepare you for the important job of grabbing defensive rebounds.

Defensive fundamentals: It is difficult to work on defensive fundamentals without someone to guard. Proper stance can be learned in front of a mirror, but you will need opposition to perfect your skills. Time spent studying defensive techniques will help you develop a good defensive state of mind so that you can concentrate on your skills on the court.

Tips

1. You can improve your game by practicing skills on your own.
2. Work on the hardest shots as well as the ones you can make easily.
3. Practice hook shots and tipping with both hands.
4. Take your time with foul shots and step away from the line after shooting twice.
5. Keep your head up whenever you dribble.
6. Practice catching as well as passing.
7. Develop a good defensive stance in front of a mirror and study defensive techniques when you cannot practice guarding an opponent.

16

THE ART OF NOT FOULING

The importance of avoiding fouls: Even a team's best player is of limited value when he has five personal fouls against him. Many coaches will bench a player with three or four fouls if it is early in the game. To be able to play an aggressive offensive and defensive game without excessive fouling is not a simple task.

Defensive fouls: The vast majority of fouls are committed while a team is playing defense. There are several reasons for this. First, the defender is usually trying to stop something that has already started, such as a player driving for the basket. Second, there is a natural tendency to use the hands on defense. Finally, most offensive players and teams try to create situations in which defensive fouls will occur.

The most common fouls committed by defense players fall into the category of illegal contact. Examples are slapping, pushing, and blocking or bumping the

GOING FOR THE BALL OFTEN CAUSES FOULS.

offensive player. When this type of contact is caused by the defense, it is a foul whether the offensive player has the ball or not. In most cases this contact is the direct result of an improper or lazy defensive effort.

Slapping usually occurs when the defender goes after the ball instead of maintaining proper position. Pushing is often an attempt to make up for failure to gain good rebounding position. Bumping a man is caused by trying to regain a position lost through relaxation or failure to maintain perfect balance. All are defensive errors.

A general rule to use in an effort to keep defensive fouling at a minimum is to keep moving your feet to

MOVE TO GET REBOUNDING POSITION AND YOU WON'T HAVE TO PUSH.

maintain proper position. A defensive player who is in position does not have to foul to prevent his man from scoring. In fact, he will often be fouled by the offensive man, who is frustrated by his inability to gain an advantage.

PROPER DEFENSIVE FOOTWORK WILL PREVENT YOU FROM COMMITTING THIS FOUL.

Offensive fouls: Offensive fouls are normally committed by dribblers, screeners, or rebounders. In all three cases fouls can be avoided by recognizing when the defensive man has established a position that will make an offensive move illegal.

Dribblers are entitled to their path unless the defense is set in that path for a full count of one. A man setting a screen must not move into a defender once he and the man he is guarding are on the move. Offensive rebounders must change their course if the defender has taken a position on the direct route to the basket.

Because of the speed at which the game is played it is impossible to avoid all contact. It is possible, though, to keep fouling to a minimum by concentrating on body control and balance. Keep in mind the situations in which fouls are most likely to occur. When in those situations strive for perfect execution. Never try to make up for a physical or mental mistake by fouling.

THIS FOUL IS ON THE OFFENSIVE MAN.

THIS FOUL IS ON THE DEFENSIVE MAN.

THIS IS A LEGAL SCREEN.

THIS IS AN ILLEGAL SCREEN; THE FOUL IS ON THE DEFENSIVE MAN.

IF A DEFENSIVE MAN TAKES AWAY THE DIRECT PATH TO THE BASKET, YOU MUST GO AROUND HIM.

Tips

1. Excessive fouling will put you on the bench.
2. Poor defensive fundamentals lead to fouling.
3. Good body position is the key to avoiding a foul.
4. Know where the defense is when you're on offense.
5. Concentrate on avoiding fouls.

17

KNOWING THE RULES

The importance of knowing the rules: A thorough knowledge of the rules is essential if you are to play any game well. Rules are not merely restrictions. In many cases, rules increase the flexibility of play by providing opportunities that might otherwise be overlooked. For example, basketball rules state that after a basket or free throw is made, the ball may be put in play anywhere along the endline. This can be very important when a team is attempting to inbounds the ball against a full-court press. In the same situation, a player is also permitted to pass to a teammate who is out of bounds. He may find that this is the only way to successfully move the ball without interception.

Any player, not only the coach or captain, may ask for a time out, but if more than five time outs are called in a game, a team will be charged with a technical foul. In a free throw situation, if a man steps over the line before the ball hits the rim, the shot will not count and must be taken again. Obviously, ignorance of the rules not only limits your ability to take full advantage of the many options of play, but also can be the cause of unnecessary penalties imposed on your team.

Some of the most important basketball rules:

1. Only five players may be on the floor at a time.
2. A substitute must report to the scorer's bench before entering a game.
3. A player may incur only five personal fouls per game.
4. A player may not leave the court without the official's permission.
5. A team is allowed five time outs per game. Any player can call time out.
6. A player is allowed only one continuous series of dribbles.
7. The ball must be moved out of the backcourt within ten seconds.
8. Once the ball is in the front court, the offensive team may not return it to the backcourt.
9. On a jump ball, only the jumpers may enter the circle before the ball is touched.
10. A player disqualifies his own foul shot by:
    a. taking longer than ten seconds to shoot
    b. stepping over the line before the ball hits the rim
    c. shooting from outside the circle

11. A player disqualifies a teammate's foul shot by:
    a. crossing the line before the ball hits the rim
    b. leaving the lane space too soon
12. An offensive player can stay in the lane area for only three seconds at a time.
13. If an official designates a player to make a throw-in from out of bounds, that player must make the throw.
14. A player taking the ball out of bounds must not step over the boundary line.
15. After a basket is made, the ball may be put in play from anywhere along the endline.
16. A player putting the ball in play from behind the endline may pass to a teammate who is out of bounds.
17. A player should avoid body contact whenever possible.
18. A player may not swing his elbows excessively for any reason.
19. A player may never enter the path of an opponent whose feet are off the ground.
20. A player should not unnecessarily delay the game.
21. It is not permissible to intentionally strike an opponent or official or to use foul language on the court.
22. Scoring errors may be corrected if brought to an official's attention immediately.

Obeying the rules: Once you have learned the rules, obey them. Never cheat, hoping you won't be caught. Instead, try to understand the spirit behind the rules and stay well within their limits. Victories won by unsportsmanlike conduct or by breaking rules are hollow victories and destroy the purpose of the game.

Tips

1. Know the rules and remember that they can provide you with opportunities you might otherwise overlook.
2. Stick strictly to the rules and try to understand the spirit behind them.
3. Never argue with an official's decision or use impolite language on the court.

HARLEY KNOSHER was born in Aurora, Illinois and received his B.S. in education at Miami University in Oxford, Ohio, where he was co-captain of the varsity basketball team. The Miami team on which he played won two Mid-American Conference Championships and twice participated in the National Collegiate Athletic Association tournament. Mr. Knosher received an M.A. from Northwestern University, where he began his coaching career, serving as freshman basketball coach for three years. Since 1960 he has been varsity basketball coach at Knox College in Galesburg, Illinois, and since 1968 he has served as athletic director for the college as well. During the period he has coached them, Knox teams have won six holiday tournament titles. Currently, Mr. Knosher spends several weeks during the summer as an instructor for All-American Sports Camps, working with boys from ten to fourteen.

LEONARD KESSLER and his wife, Ethel, have written and illustrated many popular books for young readers, including *Do Baby Bears Sit in Chairs?*, *Are You Square?*, and *The Day Daddy Stayed Home*. Mr. Kessler is also the illustrator of *Basic Baseball Strategy*. A graduate of Carnegie Institute of Technology, Mr. Kessler and his wife and children live in New City, New York.